THE MATH HANDBOOK

FOR STUDENTS WITH MATH DIFFICULTIES, DYSCALCULIA, DYSLEXIA OR ADHD
(GRADES 1-7)

HELMY FABER, MA

Universal-Publishers
Boca Raton

The Math Handbook
for Students with Math Difficulties,
Dyscalculia, Dyslexia or ADHD

Universal Publishers, Inc.
Boca Raton, Florida • USA
www.Universal-Publishers.com
2017

ISBN-10: 1-62734-106-4 (pbk.)
ISBN-13: 978-1-62734-106-6 (pbk.)

Illustrations by Drusilla Ng

Editing and Typesetting by
Educational Publishing House Pte Ltd (Singapore)

Foreword

The Math Handbook for Students with Math Difficulties, Dyscalculia, Dyslexia or ADHD has been specially developed for:

* Students who have been diagnosed with Dyscalculia; other terms may include Mathematics Learning Disability, or Mathematics Disorder.

* Students who have been diagnosed with Dyslexia; as according to research more than fifty percent of those experience difficulties with mathematics. Some students may have Dyslexia and Dyscalculia as co-existing disorders.

* Students diagnosed with ADHD; as they may struggle with mathematics. Some students may have ADHD and Dyscalculia as co-existing disorders.

* Students who have difficulties in learning Mathematics.

* Slow learners.

* Teens/Adults who have severe Math Difficulties or Dyscalculia.

Students who are struggling with Math will improve their self-confidence and independence when using the The Math Handbook for Students with Math Difficulties, Dyscalculia, Dyslexia or ADHD. It will provide them with extra support, reduce their anxiety about Math and produce better results.

This book is suitable to be used in combination with Educational Therapy or remedial intervention in Math that students with dyscalculia or Math difficulties need. An assessment conducted by a psychologist is essential and early interventions are most effective.

I would like to thank all the teachers, Allied Educators and Educational Therapists who generously provided feedback pertaining to the first edition of the MRB in Singapore. Special thanks to Dr Wong Khoon Yoong (Singapore) and Dr Steve Chinn (UK) for their feedback, supportive words and inspirational work.

Lastly, thank you to my students and their parents who provided me with invaluable feedback and information. Hopefully many others will benefit from this book and enjoy learning Math!

Helmy Faber
Developmental Psychologist
-Educational Therapist

Contents

Number Bonds of 10

				10					
								9	1
							8	2	
						7	3		
					6	4			
				5	5				
			4	6					
		3	7						
	2	8							
1	9								

Number Bonds of 10

 + 0 $10 + 0 = 10$

+ $9 + 1 = 10$

+ $8 + 2 = 10$

+ $7 + 3 = 10$

+ $6 + 4 = 10$

+ $5 + 5 = 10$

Number Bonds up to 10

2

2 + 0
1 + 1
0 + 2

3

3 + 0
2 + 1
1 + 2
0 + 3

4

4 + 0
3 + 1
2 + 2
1 + 3
0 + 4

5

5 + 0
4 + 1
3 + 2
2 + 3
1 + 4
0 + 5

6

6 + 0
5 + 1
4 + 2
3 + 3
2 + 4
1 + 5
0 + 6

for Students with Math Difficulties, Dyscalculia, Dyslexia or ADHD

7	**8**	**9**	**10**
7 + 0	8 + 0	9 + 0	10 + 0
6 + 1	7 + 1	8 + 1	9 + 1
5 + 2	6 + 2	7 + 2	8 + 2
4 + 3	5 + 3	6 + 3	7 + 3
3 + 4	4 + 4	5 + 4	6 + 4
2 + 5	3 + 5	4 + 5	5 + 5
1 + 6	2 + 6	3 + 6	4 + 6
0 + 7	1 + 7	2 + 7	3 + 7
	0 + 8	1 + 8	2 + 8
		0 + 9	1 + 9
			0 + 10

Commutative addition: 7 + 2 = 2 + 7 etc…

Addition up to 20

$10 + 10 = 20$

$11 + 9 = 20$ ➔ $9 + 11 = 20$

$12 + 8 = 20$ $8 + 12 = 20$

$13 + 7 = 20$ $7 + 13 = 20$

$14 + 6 = 20$ $6 + 14 = 20$

$15 + 5 = 20$ $5 + 15 = 20$

$16 + 4 = 20$ $4 + 16 = 20$

$17 + 3 = 20$ $3 + 17 = 20$

$18 + 2 = 20$ $2 + 18 = 20$

$19 + 1 = 20$ $1 + 19 = 20$

$20 + 0 = 20$ $0 + 20 = 20$

Basic Addition and Subtraction

+/−	1	2	3	4	5	6	7	8	9	10
1	2	3	4	5	6	7	8	9	10	11
2	3	4	5	6	7	8	9	10	11	12
3	4	5	6	7	8	9	10	11	12	13
4	5	6	7	8	9	10	11	12	13	14
5	6	7	8	9	10	11	12	13	14	15
6	7	8	9	10	11	12	13	14	15	16
7	8	9	10	11	12	13	14	15	16	17
8	9	10	11	12	13	14	15	16	17	18
9	10	11	12	13	14	15	16	17	18	19
10	11	12	13	14	15	16	17	18	19	20

Doubles

1 + 1 = 2	6 + 6 = 12
2 + 2 = 4	7 + 7 = 14
3 + 3 = 6	8 + 8 = 16
4 + 4 = 8	9 + 9 = 18
5 + 5 = 10	10 + 10 = 20
11 + 11 = 22	16 + 16 = 32
12 + 12 = 24	17 + 17 = 34
13 + 13 = 26	18 + 18 = 36
14 + 14 = 28	19 + 19 = 38
15 + 15 = 30	20 + 20 = 40

Doubling and Halving

Some examples:

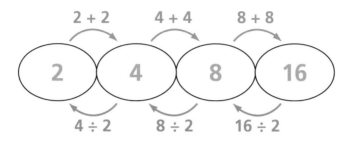

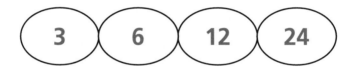

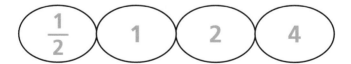

Number Line Till 20

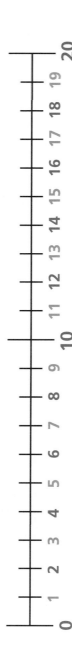

for Students with Math Difficulties, Dyscalculia, Dyslexia or ADHD

Addition and Subtraction Below 20

8 + 3 = ?

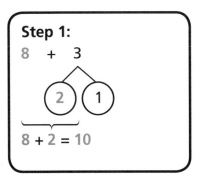

Step 1:	Step 2:
8 + 3	8 + 3
2 1	2 1
8 + 2 = 10	10 + 1 = 11

8 + 3 = 11

! Note: $8 + 3 = 3 + 8$

---

16 − 3 = ?

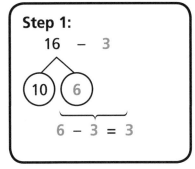 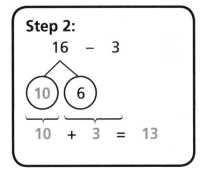

Step 1:	Step 2:
16 − 3	16 − 3
10 6	10 6
6 − 3 = 3	10 + 3 = 13

16 − 3 = 13

! Check your answer: $13 + 3 = 16$

$14 - 6 = ?$

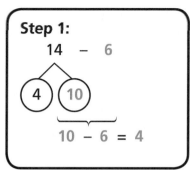

Step 1:

$$14 \quad - \quad 6$$

$$4 \quad 10$$

$$10 - 6 = 4$$

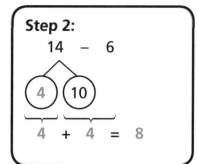

Step 2:

$$14 \quad - \quad 6$$

$$4 \quad 10$$

$$4 + 4 = 8$$

$14 - 6 = 8$

! Check your answer: $8 + 6 = 14$

Addition Using Number Line

28 + 8 = ?

$$28 + 2 = 30$$
$$30 + 6 = 36$$

20   28   30   36   40
         +2   +6

28 + 8 = 36

Subtraction Using Number Line

75 − 7 = ?

7

5

2

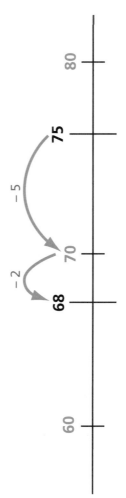

60   68   70   75   80

− 2   − 5

75 − 5 = 70. 70 − 2 = 68
! Check your answer: 68 + 7 = 75

75 − 7 = 68

Addition – Up to 2-digit Numbers

27 + 42 = ?

* Place the numbers you are going to add such that the digits in the same place values are placed in the same column (i.e. ones under ones, tens under tens, etc).

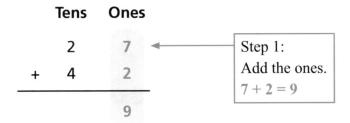

```
     Tens   Ones

       2      7   ◄────  Step 1:
  +    4      2          Add the ones.
  ─────────────          7 + 2 = 9
              9
```

```
     Tens   Ones

       2      7
  +    4      2          Step 2:
  ─────────────          Add the tens.
       6      9          2 + 4 = 6
```

Addition – Up to 4-digit Numbers

2,764 + 978 = ?

* Always place the number with more digits on top.

Thousands	Hundreds	Tens	Ones
2	7	¹6	4
+	9	7	8
			2

Step 1:
Add the ones.
$4 + 8 = 12$

Thousands	Hundreds	Tens	Ones
2	¹7	¹6	4
+	9	7	8
		4	2

Step 2:
Add the tens.
$1 + 6 + 7 = 14$

	Thousands	Hundreds	Tens	Ones
	^{1}2	^{1}7	6	4
+		9	7	8
		7	4	2

Step 3:
Add the hundreds.
$1 + 7 + 9 = 17$

	Thousands	Hundreds	Tens	Ones
	^{1}2	7	6	4
+		9	7	8
	3	7	4	2

Step 4:
Add the thousands.
$1 + 2 = 3$

Subtraction – Up to 2-digit Numbers

* Place the numbers you are going to add such that the digits in the same place values are placed in the same column. (i.e. ones under ones, tens under tens, etc)

70 – 46 = ?

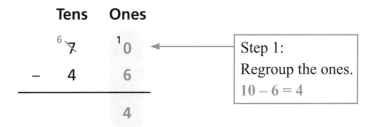

	Tens	Ones
	$^6\not7$	$^1 0$
–	4	6
		4

Step 1:
Regroup the ones.
$10 - 6 = 4$

	Tens	Ones
	$^6\not7$	0
–	4	6
	2	4

Step 2:
Subtract the tens.
$6 - 4 = 2$

! Check your answer: $24 + 46 = 70$

Subtraction – Up to 3-digit Numbers

718 − 179 = ?

Hundreds	Tens	Ones
7	⁰X̶	¹8
− 1	7	9
		9

Step 1:
Regroup the ones.
18 − 9 = 9

Hundreds	Tens	Ones
⁶X̶	¹⁰X̶	¹8
− 1	7	9
	3	9

Step 2:
Regroup the tens.
10 − 7 = 3

Hundreds	Tens	Ones
⁶X̶	¹⁰X̶	¹8
− 1	7	9
5	3	9

Step 3:
Subtract the hundreds.
6 − 1 = 5

! Check your answer: 539 + 179 = 718

Math Vocabulary (1)

Operation	Sign	Meaning	Example
Addition	+	Sum, adding, altogether, in all, more	7 + 2 = 9
Subtraction	−	Minus, difference, take out, take away, left, gave away	8 − 5 = 3
Multiplication	×	Times, adding equal groups	5 × 6 = 30
Division	÷	Sharing things equally, each get	24 ÷ 8 = 3

Sign	Meaning	Example
=	Is equal to	5 + 3 = 3 + 5
≠	Is not equal to	10 ≠ 9 + 2
>	Is greater than	6 > 3
<	Is smaller than	5 < 8

Types of Numbers	Example
Whole numbers	1, 2, 3, 4, 5, 6, 7, 8, 9, 10, 11, 12, 13, 14, 15…
Even numbers	2, 4, 6, 8, 10, 12, 14, 16, 18, 20…
Odd numbers	1, 3, 5, 7, 9, 11, 13, 15, 17, 19…
Square numbers $(1 \times 1, 2 \times 2, 3 \times 3, 4 \times 4, …)$	1, 4, 9, 16, 25, 36, 49, 64, 81…
Cube numbers $(1 \times 1 \times 1, 2 \times 2 \times 2, 3 \times 3 \times 3, 4 \times 4 \times 4, …)$	1, 8, 27, 64, 125, 216, 343, 512, 729…

Order of numbers	Meaning	Example
Ascending order	From smallest to greatest	2, 4, 8, 12
Descending order	From greatest to smallest	15, 10, 5, 2

	Meaning	Example
Quotient	The result of dividing one number by another	When dividing 6 by 2, the quotient is 3.
Remainder	What is left over after dividing	When dividing 5 by 2, the remainder is 1.
Factor	A factor of a number divides it exactly	Factors of 12: 1, 2, 3, 4, 6 and 12.
Product	The result of multiplying numbers together	Product of 6 and 9 is 54.
Prime number	A number that has exactly 2 factors, namely itself and 1	2, 3, 5, 7, 11, 13, 17, 19
Composite number	A number that has more than 2 factors	21 has 4 factors: 1, 3, 7 and 21 (Note: 1 has only 1 factor, so it is neither a prime nor a composite number)

Times Tables Key Facts

Examples

$1 \times 3 = 3$
$2 \times 3 = 3 + 3 = 6$
$5 \times 3 = 3 + 3 + 3 + 3 + 3 = 15$
$10 \times 3 = 3 + 3 + 3 + 3 + 3 + 3 + 3 + 3 + 3 + 3 = 30$

$1 \times 5 = 5$
$2 \times 5 = 5 + 5 = 10$
$5 \times 5 = 5 + 5 + 5 + 5 + 5 = 25$
$10 \times 5 = 5 + 5 + 5 + 5 + 5 + 5 + 5 + 5 + 5 + 5 = 50$

$1 \times 7 = 7$
$2 \times 7 = 7 + 7 = 14$
$5 \times 7 = 7 + 7 + 7 + 7 + 7 = 35$
$10 \times 7 = 7 + 7 + 7 + 7 + 7 + 7 + 7 + 7 + 7 + 7 = 70$

$1 \times 8 = 8$
$2 \times 8 = 8 + 8 = 16$
$5 \times 8 = 8 + 8 + 8 + 8 + 8 = 40$
$10 \times 8 = 8 + 8 + 8 + 8 + 8 + 8 + 8 + 8 + 8 + 8 = 80$

Multiplication/Division Square

×/÷	1	2	3	4	5	6	7	8	9	10
1	1	2	3	4	5	6	7	8	9	10
2	2	4	6	8	10	12	14	16	18	20
3	3	6	9	12	15	18	21	24	27	30
4	4	8	12	16	20	24	28	32	36	40
5	5	10	15	20	25	30	35	40	45	50
6	6	12	18	24	30	36	42	48	54	60
7	7	14	21	28	35	42	49	56	63	70
8	8	16	24	32	40	48	56	64	72	80
9	9	18	27	36	45	54	63	72	81	90
10	10	20	30	40	50	60	70	80	90	100

Division Darts - *Cards*

$5 \times 9 = 45$
$45 \div 9 = 5$
$45 \div 5 = 9$

$5 \times 4 = 20$
$20 \div 4 = 5$
$20 \div 5 = 4$

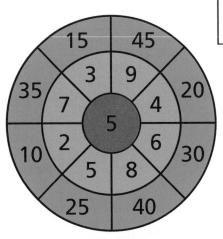

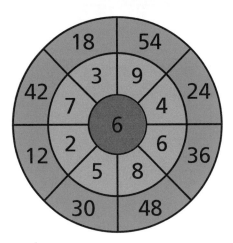

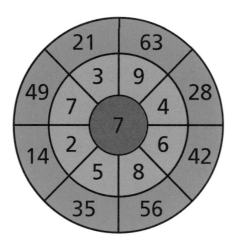

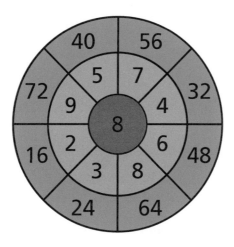

Note: $8 \times 6 = 6 \times 8$

Multiplication – 2-digit Number by a 1-digit Number

* Place the numbers you are going to multiply such that the digits in the same place values are placed in the same column. (i.e. ones under ones, tens under tens, etc)
* Always place the greater number on top of the smaller number.

$57 \times 4 = ?$

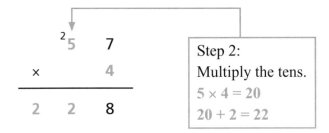

$$
\begin{array}{r}
{}^{2}5 \quad 7 \\
\times \qquad 4 \\
\hline
8
\end{array}
$$

Step 1:
Multiply the ones.
$7 \times 4 = 28$

$$
\begin{array}{r}
{}^{2}5 \quad 7 \\
\times \qquad 4 \\
\hline
2 \quad 2 \quad 8
\end{array}
$$

Step 2:
Multiply the tens.
$5 \times 4 = 20$
$20 + 2 = 22$

Multiplication – 2-digit Number by a 2-digit Number

57 × 34 = ?

Continuing from the previous page:

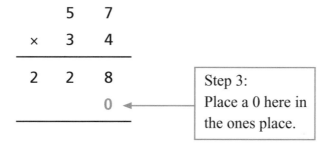

Step 3:
Place a 0 here in the ones place.

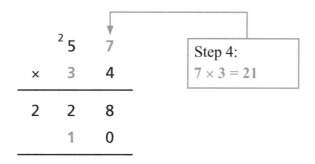

Step 4:
7 × 3 = 21

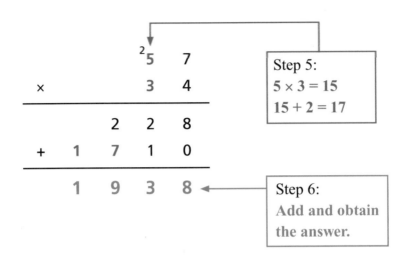

$$\begin{array}{r} {}^{2}5\ \ 7 \\ \times\ \ \ \ 3\ \ 4 \\ \hline 2\ \ 2\ \ 8 \\ +\ 1\ \ 7\ \ 1\ \ 0 \\ \hline 1\ \ 9\ \ 3\ \ 8 \end{array}$$

Step 5:
$5 \times 3 = 15$
$15 + 2 = 17$

Step 6:
Add and obtain the answer.

! Check your answer: Steps 1 to 6

©2017 Helmy Faber, *The Math Handbook*

Multiplication – 2-digit Number by a 2-digit Number

Thousands	Hundreds	Tens	Ones
		7	4
		× 2	6
	¹ 4	2	4
		2	0
		8	0
+ 1	4	0	0
1	9	2	4

$6 \times 4 = 24$

$6 \times 70 = 420$

$20 \times 4 = 80$

$20 \times 70 = 1400$

Division Rules

A number can be divided (in whole numbers) by:

* 2   if the last digit is even

   Example: 824   (4 is even)

* 3   if the sum of the digits are divisible by 3

   Example: 375
   Sum of digits = 3 + 7 + 5 = 15
   15 ÷ 3 = 5
   So 375 ÷ 3 = 125

* 4   if the last 2 digits are divisible by 4

   Example: 2,5**84**
   84 can be divided by 4
   So 2,584 ÷ 4 = 646

* 5   if the last digit is a 5 or a 0

   Example: 57**5** ÷ 5 = 115

* 9   if the sum of the digits are divisible by 9

   Example: 28,575
   Sum of digits = 2 + 8 + 5 + 7 + 5 = 27
   27 ÷ 9 = 3
   So 28,575 ÷ 9 = 3175

Division – 2-digit Number by 1-digit Number

$$\begin{array}{r} 4 \\ 4 \overline{\smash{)}\ 1\ 6} \\ \underline{1\ 6} \\ 0 \end{array}$$

16 ÷ 4 = 4   ! Check your answer: 4 × 4 = 16

$$\begin{array}{r} 5\ \text{R2} \\ 4 \overline{\smash{)}\ 2\ 2} \\ \underline{2\ 0} \\ 2 \end{array}$$

5 × 4 = 20

22 ÷ 4 = 5 R2 ! Check your answer: 4 × 5 = 20. 20 + 2 = 22

Division – 3-digit Number by 1-digit Number

$2{,}148 \div 4 = ?$

```
        5  3  7
   ┌─────────────
 4 │  2  1  4  8
      2  0 ┊     ┊        4 × 5 < 21
      ─────▼     ┊
         1  4    ┊
         1  2    ┊        4 × 3 < 14
         ───────▼
            2  8
            2  8          4 × 7 = 28
            ─────
               0
```

So $2{,}148 \div 4 = 537$! Check your answer: $537 \times 4 = 2{,}148$

Multiplication and Division by Powers of 10

Multiplication

10 × 24 = 240   (Insert 0)

100 × 36 = 3,600   (Insert 00)

1000 × 18 = 18,000   (Insert 000)

Division

3,900 ÷ 10 = 390   (Cancel 0)

3,600 ÷ 100 = 36   (Cancel 00)

29,000 ÷ 1000 = 29   (Cancel 000)

Round Off

* Rounding off to the nearest ten (10)

526 ☐→ 5<u>2</u>6   underline the digit in the tens
⬆   place

> The digit 2 is in the tens place.
> We need to determine whether to
> round **down** to **20** or round **up** to **30**.

If the digit in the ones place is ≥ 5, round up,
i.e. add 1 to the digit in the tens place.

If the digit is ≤ 4, round down, i.e. the digit in
the tens place remains the same.

6 > 5 ☐→ 526 ≈ **530**

So 526 rounded off to the nearest 10 is 530.

* Rounding off to the nearest hundred (100)

3,<u>8</u>51   ☐→ 3,900
29,<u>4</u>41 ☐→ 29,400
4,<u>0</u>62   ☐→ 4,100

Numbers till 100

1	one	11	eleven	30	thirty
2	two	12	twelve	40	forty
3	three	13	thirteen	50	fifty
4	four	14	fourteen	60	sixty
5	five	15	fifteen	70	seventy
6	six	16	sixteen	80	eighty
7	seven	17	seventeen	90	ninety
8	eight	18	eighteen	100	one hundred
9	nine	19	nineteen		
10	ten	20	twenty		

1,000	one thousand
10,000	ten thousand
100,000	one hundred thousand
1,000,000	one million

Ordinal Numbers

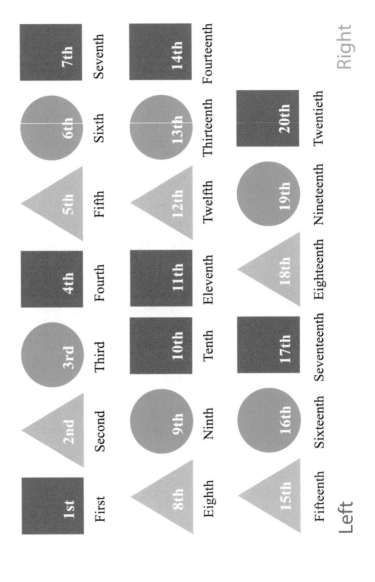

1st	2nd	3rd	4th	5th	6th	7th
First	Second	Third	Fourth	Fifth	Sixth	Seventh
8th	9th	10th	11th	12th	13th	14th
Eighth	Ninth	Tenth	Eleventh	Twelfth	Thirteenth	Fourteenth
15th	16th	17th	18th	19th	20th	
Fifteenth	Sixteenth	Seventeenth	Eighteenth	Nineteenth	Twentieth	

Left

Right

Place Value (1)

768,935

hundred thousands	ten thousands	thousands	hundreds	tens	ones
7	6	8,	9	3	5
700,000	60,000	8,000	900	30	5

Seven hundred and sixty-eight thousand, nine hundred and thirty-five

Place Value (2)

43,249,577

ten millions	millions	hundred thousands	ten thousands	thousands	hundreds	tens	ones
4	3,	2	4	9,	5	7	7
40,000,000	3,000,000	200,000	40,000	9,000	500	70	7

Forty-three million, two hundred and forty-nine thousand, five hundred and seventy-seven

Place Value (3)

635.298

hundreds	tens	ones	.	tenths	hundredths	thousandths
6	3	5	.	2	9	8
600	30	5		0.2	0.09	0.008

two tenths
nine hundredths
eight thousandths

Table of Conversion for Fractions, Decimals and Percentages

Fraction	Decimal	Percentage
$\frac{1}{1} = 1$	1	100%
$\frac{1}{2}$	0.5	50%
$\frac{1}{3}$	0.33	33.3%
$\frac{1}{4}$	0.25	25%
$\frac{1}{5}$	0.2	20%
$\frac{1}{6}$	0.167	16.7%
$\frac{1}{7}$	0.143	14.3%
$\frac{1}{8}$	0.125	12.5%
$\frac{1}{9}$	0.11	11.1%
$\frac{1}{10}$	0.1	10%

Fractions

A fraction describes a part of a whole.

Example: $\frac{1}{6}$ of a pizza.

A fraction comprises of a numerator (the top number) and the denominator (the bottom number).

The denominator indicates the number of equal parts there are.

Example: We know that the pizza is divided into 6 equal slices as the denominator is 6.

The greater the denominator, the smaller each part is.

Example: The more equal pieces a pizza is being sliced, the smaller each slice will become.

From greatest to smallest:

$$\frac{1}{2}, \frac{1}{3}, \frac{1}{4}, \frac{1}{5}, \frac{1}{6}, \frac{1}{7}, \frac{1}{8} \cdots$$

Half $= \frac{1}{2}$ Quarter $= \frac{1}{4}$

Basic Fractions (1)

Half and half make one whole.

$$\frac{1}{2} + \frac{1}{2} = \frac{2}{2} = 1$$

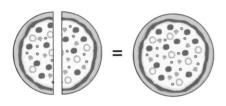

$$1 - \frac{1}{2} = \frac{1}{2}$$

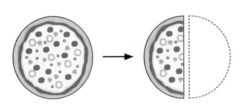

Basic Fractions (2)

One third and two thirds make one whole.

$$\frac{1}{3} + \frac{2}{3} = \frac{3}{3} = 1$$

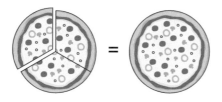

$$1 - \frac{1}{3} = \frac{2}{3}$$

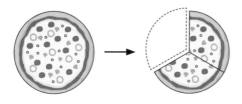

Basic Fractions (3)

One quarter (or one fourth) and three quarters make one whole.

$$\frac{1}{4} + \frac{3}{4} = \frac{4}{4} = 1$$

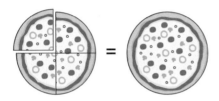

> **Note:**
> $\frac{1}{4} + \frac{1}{4} = \frac{2}{4} = \frac{1}{2}$ Two quarters equal to half

$$1 - \frac{1}{4} = \frac{3}{4}$$

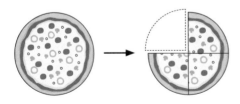

Basic Fractions (4)

One fifth and four fifths make one whole.

$$\frac{1}{5} + \frac{4}{5} = \frac{5}{5} = 1$$

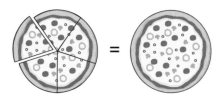

$$1 - \frac{2}{5} = \frac{3}{5}$$

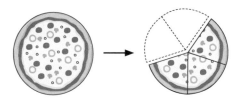

Addition of Fractions (1)

When two fractions have the same denominators, the numerators can be directly added together.

$$\frac{1}{5} + \frac{3}{5} = ?$$

$$\frac{1}{5} \quad + \quad \frac{3}{5} \quad = \quad \frac{4}{5}$$

$$\frac{1}{5} + \frac{3}{5} = \frac{4}{5} \qquad \text{Just add the numerators together}$$

Addition of Fractions (2)

Adding with the same denominator (bottom)

$$\frac{4}{5} + \frac{4}{5} = ?$$

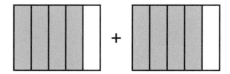

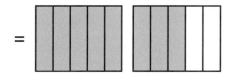

$$\frac{4}{5} + \frac{4}{5} = \frac{8}{5} = 1\frac{3}{5}$$

! Always convert improper fractions to a mixed number.

Addition of Fractions (3) – Different Denominators

Example 1:

$$\frac{1}{3} + \frac{1}{2} = ?$$

First, convert the fractions to the same denominator. This can be done by finding a common multiple.

Next, convert both fractions to the same denominator.

$$\frac{1}{3} \xrightarrow{\times 2} = \frac{2}{6} \quad \frac{1}{2} \xrightarrow{\times 3} = \frac{3}{6}$$

Then we can add the fractions:

$$\frac{2}{6} + \frac{3}{6} = \frac{5}{6}$$

Example 2:

$$\frac{5}{9} + \frac{5}{6} = ?$$

Step 1: Look for the common multiple.

$1 \times 9 = 9$	$1 \times 6 = 6$
$2 \times 9 = 18$	$2 \times 6 = 12$
$3 \times 9 = 27$	$3 \times 6 = 18$

Step 2: Convert both fractions to the same denominator.

$$\frac{5}{9} = \frac{10}{18} \qquad \text{and} \qquad \frac{5}{6} = \frac{15}{18}$$

$$\frac{5}{9} + \frac{5}{6} = \frac{10}{18} + \frac{15}{18}$$

$$= \frac{25}{18}$$

! Always convert improper fractions to a mixed number.

$$= 1\frac{7}{18}$$

Addition of Mixed Numbers (1)

$$3\frac{1}{4} + 1\frac{7}{8} = ?$$

Step 1: Add the whole numbers.

$$3 + 1 = 4$$

Step 2: Add the fractions.

$$\frac{1}{4} + \frac{7}{8} = \frac{2}{8} + \frac{7}{8}$$! Always convert into the same denominator

$$= \frac{9}{8}$$! Always convert improper fractions to a mixed number.

$$= 1\frac{1}{8}$$

Step 3: Add fractions together with the whole numbers.

$$4 + 1\frac{1}{8} = 5\frac{1}{8}$$

So $3\frac{1}{4} + 1\frac{7}{8} = 5\frac{1}{8}$

Addition of Mixed Numbers (2)

The addition of $3\frac{1}{4} + 1\frac{7}{8}$ can also be represented as follows:

Step 1:

Step 2:

Step 3:

Subtraction of Fractions

When the denominators are the same, the numerators can be subtracted directly.

$$\frac{7}{10} - \frac{4}{10} = ?$$

$$\frac{7}{10} \quad - \quad \frac{4}{10} \quad = \quad \frac{3}{10}$$

! Check your answer: $\frac{3}{10} + \frac{4}{10} = \frac{7}{10}$

Subtraction of Fractions (1) – Different Denominators

Example:

$$\frac{4}{5} - \frac{1}{3} = ?$$

First, convert the fractions to the same denominator. This can be done by finding a common multiple.

Next, convert both fractions to the same denominator.

$$\frac{1}{3} = \frac{5}{15}$$

Next, subtract the fractions.

$$\frac{12}{15} - \frac{5}{15} = \frac{7}{15}$$

! Check your answer: $\frac{7}{15} + \frac{5}{15} = \frac{12}{15} = \frac{4}{5}$

Subtraction of Fractions (2) – Different Denominators

The subtraction of $\frac{4}{5} - \frac{1}{3}$ can also be represented as follows:

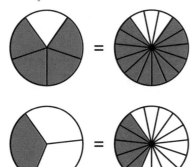

©2017 Helmy Faber, *The Math Handbook*

Subtraction of Mixed Numbers

Treat the whole numbers separately from the fractions.

(1) If the first fraction is greater, subtract accordingly.

$$
\begin{array}{r}
2\frac{1}{2} \\
-\ \ \frac{1}{2} \\
\hline
2
\end{array}
\qquad
\begin{array}{r}
3\frac{3}{5} \\
-\ \ \frac{2}{5} \\
\hline
3\frac{1}{5}
\end{array}
\qquad
\begin{array}{r}
5\frac{4}{9} \\
-\ 5\frac{2}{9} \\
\hline
\frac{2}{9}
\end{array}
$$

(2) If the second fraction is greater, use the whole number belonging to the first mixed number to convert it into a fraction.

$$5\frac{1}{3} - 3\frac{2}{3} = ?$$

$$5 = 4 + \frac{3}{3}$$

$$4 + \frac{3}{3} + \frac{1}{3} - 3\frac{2}{3} = 1\frac{2}{3}$$

$$\frac{4}{3} - \frac{2}{3} = \frac{2}{3}$$

$$5\frac{1}{3} - 3\frac{2}{3} = 1\frac{2}{3}$$

! Check your answer: $1\frac{2}{3} + 3\frac{2}{3} = 5\frac{1}{3}$

Math Vocabulary (2)

Term	Meaning	Example
Fraction	One or more parts of a unit or whole It is a number between 0 and 1 that is formed by dividing a number by a bigger number.	7 is called 'numerator' (top) $\dfrac{7}{8}$ 8 is called 'denominator' (bottom)
Convert fractions	Change fractions	See page 53.
Equivalent fractions	Fractions that are equal in size	$\dfrac{1}{2}, \dfrac{2}{4}, \dfrac{3}{6}, \dfrac{4}{8}, \dfrac{5}{10}$ etc…

Math Vocabulary (2)

Term	Meaning	Example
Improper fraction	Fraction where the numerator is bigger than the denominator; they are also called 'top-heavy' fractions	$\frac{7}{4}$
Mixed number	A number that has a whole number part and a fraction	$2\frac{3}{4}$ or $5\frac{1}{5}$
Common denominator	A denominator that allows two or more fractions to be written with the same denominator	The common denominators for $\frac{3}{4}$ and $\frac{5}{6}$ are 12, 24, 36, etc.
Lowest common denominator	The smallest of the common denominators	In previous example that would be 12.
Reciprocal	The number formed by turning a fraction upside down	The reciprocal of $\frac{3}{4}$ is $\frac{4}{3}$.

Fractions (1)

1

| $\frac{1}{2}$ | $\frac{1}{2}$ |

| $\frac{1}{4}$ | $\frac{1}{4}$ | $\frac{1}{4}$ | $\frac{1}{4}$ |

| $\frac{1}{8}$ | $\frac{1}{8}$ | $\frac{1}{8}$ | $\frac{1}{8}$ | $\frac{1}{8}$ | $\frac{1}{8}$ | $\frac{1}{8}$ | $\frac{1}{8}$ |

Fractions (2)

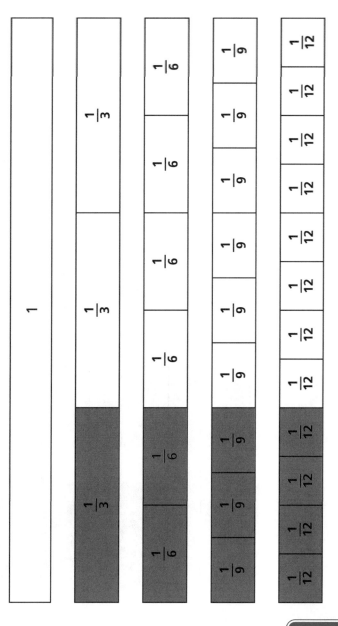

Fractions (3)

1			

$\frac{1}{5}$	$\frac{1}{5}$	$\frac{1}{5}$	$\frac{1}{5}$	$\frac{1}{5}$

$\frac{1}{10}$	$\frac{1}{10}$	$\frac{1}{10}$	$\frac{1}{10}$	$\frac{1}{10}$	$\frac{1}{10}$	$\frac{1}{10}$	$\frac{1}{10}$	$\frac{1}{10}$	$\frac{1}{10}$

$\frac{1}{20}$	$\frac{1}{20}$	$\frac{1}{20}$	$\frac{1}{20}$	$\frac{1}{20}$	$\frac{1}{20}$	$\frac{1}{20}$	$\frac{1}{20}$	$\frac{1}{20}$	$\frac{1}{20}$	$\frac{1}{20}$	$\frac{1}{20}$	$\frac{1}{20}$	$\frac{1}{20}$	$\frac{1}{20}$	$\frac{1}{20}$	$\frac{1}{20}$	$\frac{1}{20}$	$\frac{1}{20}$	$\frac{1}{20}$

Simplifying Fractions

Divide the top (numerator) and the bottom (denominator) of the fraction by the same number.

$$\frac{3}{9} = \frac{3 \div 3}{9 \div 3} = \frac{1}{3}$$

$$\frac{5}{10} = \frac{5 \div 5}{10 \div 5} = \frac{1}{2}$$

$$\frac{8}{20} = \frac{8 \div 4}{20 \div 4} = \frac{2}{5}$$

$$\frac{15}{24} = \frac{15 \div 3}{24 \div 3} = \frac{5}{8}$$

! Always check if the fraction can be simplified

Equivalent Fractions (1)

Fractions are equivalent if they have the same value, but may have different numerators and denominators.

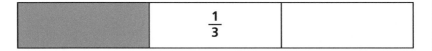

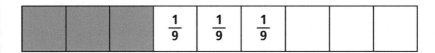

$$\frac{1}{3} = \frac{2}{6} = \frac{3}{9} = \frac{4}{12}$$

Equivalent Fractions (2)

To find equivalent fractions, multiply the top (numerator) and the bottom (denominator) by the same number.

$$\frac{1}{3} \quad \begin{matrix} \nearrow \times 2 \\ \searrow \times 2 \end{matrix} \quad = \frac{1 \times 2}{3 \times 2} = \frac{2}{6}$$

$$\frac{1}{3} \quad \begin{matrix} \nearrow \times 3 \\ \searrow \times 3 \end{matrix} \quad = \frac{1 \times 3}{3 \times 3} = \frac{3}{9}$$

$$\frac{1}{3} \quad \begin{matrix} \nearrow \times 4 \\ \searrow \times 4 \end{matrix} \quad = \frac{1 \times 4}{3 \times 4} = \frac{4}{12}$$

$$\frac{1}{3} = \frac{2}{6} = \frac{3}{9} = \frac{4}{12}$$

Comparing Fractions

(1) When comparing fractions, make sure the denominators are the same.

Example:
Which is the smallest fraction: $\frac{7}{12}$, $\frac{5}{12}$, $\frac{4}{12}$ or $\frac{3}{12}$?

$\frac{1}{12}$	$\frac{1}{12}$	$\frac{1}{12}$	$\frac{1}{12}$	$\frac{1}{12}$	$\frac{1}{12}$	$\frac{1}{12}$	$\frac{1}{12}$	$\frac{1}{12}$	$\frac{1}{12}$	$\frac{1}{12}$	$\frac{1}{12}$

The smallest fraction is $\frac{3}{12}$.

(2) When comparing fractions where the denominator is different: first convert to the same denominator, then compare.

Example:
Which is bigger: $\frac{5}{8}$ or $\frac{3}{5}$?

$$\frac{5}{8} = \frac{25}{40} \quad \text{and} \quad \frac{3}{5} = \frac{24}{40}$$

The bigger fraction is $\frac{5}{8}$.

Multiplying Fractions (1)

Multiply a fraction by a whole number; multiply the whole number with the numerator of the fraction:

$$3 \times \frac{2}{9} = ?$$

$$3 \times \frac{2}{9} = 3 \times \frac{2}{9} = \frac{6}{9} \longrightarrow \text{always simplify to } \frac{2}{3}$$

$$3 \times \frac{2}{9} = \frac{2}{9} + \frac{2}{9} + \frac{2}{9} = \frac{6}{9} = \frac{2}{3}$$

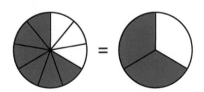

$$3 \times \frac{2}{9} = \frac{2}{3}$$

Multiplying Fractions (2)

When multipling a fraction with another fraction, first multiply both numerators then multiply both denominators.

$$\frac{1}{3} \times \frac{1}{2} = ?$$

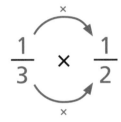

$$\frac{1}{3} \times \frac{1}{2} = \frac{1}{6}$$

Multiplying Fractions (3)

$$4\frac{1}{2} \times 4\frac{3}{4} = ?$$

Step 1: $4\frac{1}{2} \times 4 = 16\frac{4}{2} = 18$

$\frac{4}{2} = 2$

Step 2: $4\frac{1}{2} \times \frac{3}{4} = ?$

Convert $4\frac{1}{2}$ to $\frac{9}{2}$

$\frac{9}{2} \times \frac{3}{4} = \frac{27}{8}$

$\frac{27}{8} = 3\frac{3}{8}$

Step 3: $18 + 3\frac{3}{8} = 21\frac{3}{8}$

Dividing Fractions

When dividing fractions, always multiply the number/fraction on the right with its reciprocal.

$\dfrac{3}{5} \div 9 = ?$

$9 = \dfrac{9}{1}$

$\dfrac{3}{5} \div \dfrac{9}{1}$

The reciprocal of $\dfrac{9}{1} = \dfrac{1}{9}$

$= \dfrac{3}{5} \times \dfrac{1}{9} = \dfrac{3 \times 1}{5 \times 9} = \dfrac{3}{45}$ simplify to $\dfrac{1}{15}$

! Check your answer: $\dfrac{1}{15} \times 9 = \dfrac{9}{15} = \dfrac{3}{5}$

$\dfrac{2}{5} \div \dfrac{1}{6} = ?$

$\dfrac{2}{5} \times \dfrac{6}{1} = \dfrac{2 \times 6}{5 \times 1} = \dfrac{12}{5} = 2\dfrac{2}{5}$

! Check your answer: $\dfrac{12}{5} \times \dfrac{1}{6}$, simplify to $\dfrac{2}{5}$

$$4\frac{1}{4} \div 2\frac{1}{4} = ?$$

Step 1: Convert the mixed numbers to improper fractions.

$$4\frac{1}{4} = \frac{17}{4}$$

$$2\frac{1}{4} = \frac{9}{4}$$

Step 2: Multiply with the improper fraction on the right using its reciprocal.

$$\frac{17}{4} \times \frac{4}{9} = \frac{17 \times 4}{4 \times 9} = \frac{68}{36}$$

Step 3: Reduce the answer to simplest form.

$$\frac{68}{36} = 1\frac{32}{36}$$

$$= 1\frac{8}{9}$$

! Check your answer: $1\frac{8}{9} \times 2\frac{1}{4} = 4\frac{1}{4}$

Fractions (4)

What is $\frac{1}{3}$ of 18?

$18 \div 3 = 6$

$\frac{1}{3}$ of $18 = 6$

Fractions (5)

What is $\frac{4}{5}$ of 40?

$40 \div 5 = 8$ $\frac{1}{5}$ of $40 = 8$

$\frac{4}{5}$ of $40 = 8 + 8 + 8 + 8 = 4 \times 8 = 32$

Decimals

Similar to fractions, decimals are also part of a whole.

$.1 \quad = \dfrac{1}{10}$ one tenth   (1 digit after the decimal point)

$.5 \quad = \dfrac{5}{10}$ five tenths

(2 digits after the decimal point)

$.01 \quad = \dfrac{1}{100}$ one hundredth

$.06 \quad = \dfrac{6}{100}$ six hundredths

$.27 \quad = \dfrac{27}{100} = \dfrac{2}{10} + \dfrac{7}{100}$

(3 digits after the decimal point)

$.001 \quad = \dfrac{1}{1000}$ one thousandth

$.408 \quad = \dfrac{408}{1000} = \dfrac{4}{10} + \dfrac{8}{1000}$

$.379 \quad = \dfrac{379}{1000} = \dfrac{3}{10} + \dfrac{7}{100} + \dfrac{9}{1000}$

Decimals

1									
0.5					0.5				
0.333			0.333			0.333			
0.25		0.25		0.25			0.25		
0.2		0.2		0.2		0.2		0.2	
0.167	0.167		0.167		0.167		0.167		0.167
0.143	0.143	0.143		0.143	0.143		0.143	0.143	0.143
0.125	0.125	0.125	0.125	0.125	0.125	0.125	0.125		
0.111	0.111	0.111	0.111	0.111	0.111	0.111	0.111	0.111	
0.1	0.1	0.1	0.1	0.1	0.1	0.1	0.1	0.1	0.1

Decimals

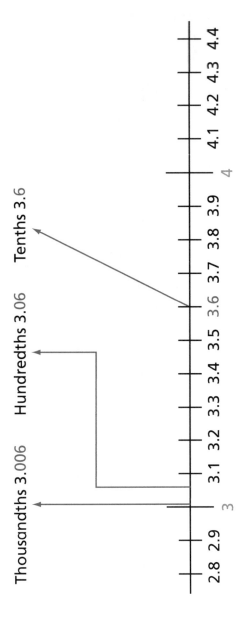

Thousandths 3.006   Hundredths 3.06   Tenths 3.6

2.8 2.9   3   3.1 3.2 3.3 3.4 3.5 3.6 3.7 3.8 3.9   4   4.1 4.2 4.3 4.4

74

Decimals: Converting Decimals into Fractions

	$\frac{1}{10}$	$\frac{1}{100}$	$\frac{1}{1000}$	
0.1	.1			$\frac{1}{10}$
0.23	.2	3		$\frac{23}{100}$
0.07	.0	7		$\frac{7}{100}$
0.239	.2	3	9	$\frac{239}{1000}$
0.045	.0	4	5	$\frac{45}{1000}$
0.307	.3	0	7	$\frac{307}{1000}$
0.008	.0	0	8	$\frac{8}{1000}$

Multiplying Decimals

$1 \div 10 = \dfrac{1}{10} = 0.1$ (tenths)

$10 \times 0.1 = 1$

$100 \times 0.1 = 10$

$1 \div 100 = \dfrac{1}{100} = 0.01$ (hundredths)

$10 \times 0.01 = 0.1$

$100 \times 0.01 = 1$ $100 = 10 \times 10$

$1 \div 1000 = \dfrac{1}{1000} = 0.001$ (thousandths)

$10 \times 0.001 = 0.01$

$100 \times 0.001 = 0.1$

$1000 \times 0.001 = 1$ $1000 = 10 \times 10 \times 10$

Multiplication/Division of Decimals by Powers of 10

$10 \times 34.285 = 342.85$

$100 \times 34.285 = 3,428.5$

$1000 \times 34.285 = 34,285$

When multiplying a decimal by 10, the decimal point will move one place to the right. Likewise when the decimal is multiplied by 100 or 1000, the decimal point will move the required places to the right. The result will always be bigger than the original number.

$45,279 \div 10 = 4,527.9$

$45,279 \div 100 = 452.79$

$45,279 \div 1000 = 45.279$

When dividing by 10 the decimal point will move one place to the left. Likewise when the decimal is divided by 100 or 1000, the decimal point will move the required places to the left. The result will always be smaller than the original number.

Converting Fractions to Decimals (1)

Convert fractions to either tenths $\left(\frac{1}{10}\right)$, hundredths $\left(\frac{1}{100}\right)$ or thousandths $\left(\frac{1}{1000}\right)$, depending on the denominator (the bottom number) of the fraction.

$$\frac{3}{5} = \frac{3 \times 2}{5 \times 2} = \frac{6}{10} = 0.6$$

tenths have 1 decimal place

$$\frac{3}{4} = \frac{3 \times 25}{4 \times 25} = \frac{75}{100} = 0.75$$

hundredths have 2 decimals places

$$\frac{3}{8} = \frac{3 \times 125}{8 \times 125} = \frac{375}{1000} = 0.375$$

thousandths have 3 decimals places

$$\frac{7}{20} = \frac{7 \times 5}{20 \times 5} = \frac{35}{100} = 0.35$$

Converting Fractions to Decimals (2)

Convert $\frac{8}{20}$ to a decimal using a traditional or talking calculator.

$8 \div 20 = 0.4$

Or use long division:

Convert $\frac{5}{7}$ to a decimal.

$$
\begin{array}{r}
0.7\ 1\ 4\ 2 \\
7\ \overline{)\ 5.0\ 0\ 0} \\
-\ 4\ 9 \\
\hline
1\ 0 \\
-\ 7 \\
\hline
3\ 0 \\
-\ 2\ 8 \\
\hline
2\ 0
\end{array}
$$

Round off answer to 3 decimal places:

$0.7142 \approx 0.714$

$\frac{5}{7} \approx 0.714$

Conversion of Decimals and Fractions

Fraction	Decimal
$\frac{1}{1}$	1
$\frac{1}{2}$	0.5
$\frac{1}{3}$	0.333
$\frac{1}{4}$	0.25
$\frac{1}{5}$	0.2
$\frac{1}{6}$	0.167
$\frac{1}{7}$	0.143
$\frac{1}{8}$	0.125
$\frac{1}{9}$	0.111
$\frac{1}{10}$	0.1

©2017 Helmy Faber, *The Math Handbook*

Addition of Decimals

Always **align the decimal point in the same position** when adding/subtracting decimals.

2.49 + 3 = ?

```
    2 . 4 9
  + 3 . 0 0
  ─────────
    5 . 4 9
```

! Check that 3 = 3.00 and put the decimals right under each other

---

34.04 + 4.841 = ?

```
    3 4 . 0 4 0
  +    4 . 8 4 1
  ───────────────
    3 8 . 8 8 1
```

! Check by adding whole numbers, then the decimals

Subtraction of Decimals

$4 - 2.34 = ?$

```
    4 . 0  0                    4 = 4.00
  - 2 . 3  4
  ─────────────
    1 . 6  6        ! Check your answer: 1.66 + 2.34 = 4
```

$75.34 - 3.125 = ?$

```
  7  5 . 3  4  0
  -     3 . 1  2  5
  ──────────────────
  7  2 . 2  1  5
            ! Check your answer: 72.215 + 3.125 = 75.340
```

$27.36 - 3.6 = ?$

```
  2  7 . 3  6
  -     3 . 6  0
  ──────────────
  2  3 . 7  6
            ! Check your answer: 23.76 + 3.60 = 27.36
```

Multiplication of Decimals by Decimals

When multiplying decimals by decimals, take note of where to put the decimal point is to be placed for the final answer.

```
    0 . 7        1
×   0 . 6        1      add the decimal places
                       together (1 + 1); the answer
    0 . 4 2      2      will have 2 decimal places
```

```
    2 . 5          1
×   3 . 0 3        2      (1 + 2); the answer will have
                         3 decimal places
    7 . 5 7 5      3
```

```
    3 . 0 7                2
×   1 . 0 0 0 9            4      (2 + 4); the answer
                                 will have 6 decimal
    3 . 0 7 2 7 6 3        6      places
```

Division of Decimals

$28.5 \div 0.3 = ?$

Multiply both numbers by 10, then divide.

$28.5 \times 10 = 285$

$0.3 \times 10 = 3$

$285 \div 3 = 95$

! Check: $95 \times 0.3 = 28.5$

$0.684 \div 0.06 = ?$

Multiply both numbers by 100, then divide.

$0.684 \times 100 = 68.4$

$0.06 \times 100 = 6$

$68.4 \div 6 = 11.4$

! Check: $11.4 \times 0.06 = 0.684$

Percentages

Percents are hundredths, so 1 percent means 1 out of 100. They can be converted from fractions and decimals.

ones	$\frac{1}{10}$	$\frac{1}{100}$	$\frac{1}{1000}$	
0	.0	1		= 1%
0	.0	5		= 5%
0	.1	0		= 10%
0	.2	5		= 25%
0	.3	3		= 33%
0	.3	7	5	= 37.5%
0	.4	5		= 45%
0	.5	0		= 50%
0	.7	5		= 75%
0	.8	8		= 88%
0	.9	9		= 99%
3	.7	6		= 376%

Percentages

100%									
50%					50%				
33.3%			33.3%			33.3%			
25%		25%		25%		25%			
20%	20%		20%		20%		20%		
16.7%	16.7%	16.7%	16.7%	16.7%	16.7%				
14.3%	14.3%	14.3%	14.3%	14.3%	14.3%	14.3%			
12.5%	12.5%	12.5%	12.5%	12.5%	12.5%	12.5%	12.5%		
11.1%	11.1%	11.1%	11.1%	11.1%	11.1%	11.1%	11.1%	11.1%	
10%	10%	10%	10%	10%	10%	10%	10%	10%	10%

Conversions of Percentages and Fractions

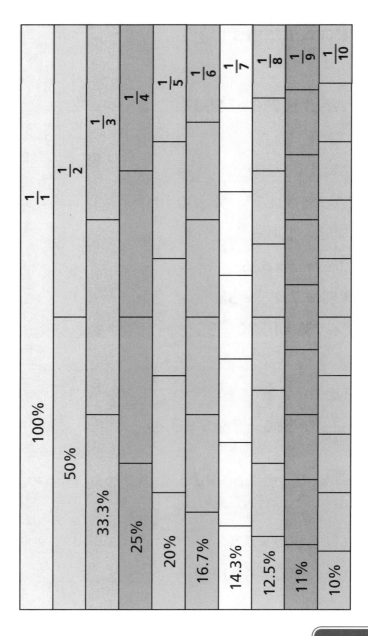

Percentages (1)

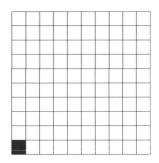

What is 7% of 500?

Method 1

Work out 1% of 500 first:

$500 \div 100 = 5$

$7\% = 7 \times 1\%$

$7\% = 7 \times 5 = 35$

So 7% of 500 = 35

Method 2

$\dfrac{7}{1\cancel{0}\cancel{0}} \times 5\cancel{0}\cancel{0} = 7 \times 5 = 35$

On the traditional or talking calculator, there are 2 ways to do this:

(1) 500 × 7%   (! Do not press =)

(2) 500 ÷ 100 × 7 =

Percentages (2)

A shirt is selling at a discount of 20%. The usual price is $69. What is the price after discount?

Step 1:   100% − 20% = 80%
          Only 80% of the original price needs to be paid.

Step 2:   Work out 1% first. $69 ÷ 100 = $0.69
          1% of $69 = $0.69

Step 3:   80% = 80 × $0.69 = $55.20

> ! Check your answer: discount means the new price should be lower than the old price

On the traditional or talking calculator:

69 − 20%   (! Do not press =)

Percentages (3)

In a class, 14 out of 42 students have blue eyes. What percentage of the students have blue eyes?

Step 1: Find the fraction, in this case $\frac{14}{42}$.

Step 2: Simplify $\frac{14}{42}$ to $\frac{1}{3}$.

Step 3: Convert the fraction into a decimal.
$$\frac{1}{3} = 0.333$$

Step 4: Convert decimal into percentage.
Multiply by 100.
$0.333 \times 100 = 33.3\%$

On the traditional or talking calculator:

$14 \div 42 = \ldots \times 100 =$

Percentages (4)

A shop selling electric appliances is offering 20% discount on a blender. The price after discount is $160. What is the original price of the blender?

Step 1: Find the percentage that the blender is selling at now.
100% − 20% = 80%

Step 2: Divide the new price by the % that is left.
$160 ÷ 80 = $2, so 1% = $2

Step 3: Calculate 100%, which is the original price.
100 × $2 = $200

The original price of the blender is $200.

! Check your answer: 1% of 200 = 2.
20% = 2 × 20 = 40. 200 − 40 = 160

Percentages (5)

What is 20% of 180?

Step 1: 10% of 180 = 180 ÷ 10 = 18

Step 2: 18 × 2 = 36
         20% of 180 = 36

What is 150% of $98?

Method 1: $\frac{150}{100}$ × $98 = $147

Method 2: 100% of 98 = 98,   50% = $\frac{1}{2}$
           $1\frac{1}{2}$ × $98 = $98 + $49 = $147

On the traditional or talking calculator:

98 × 150%   (! Do not press =)

Time

1 day	= 24 hours
1 hour	= 60 minutes
1 hour	= 4 quarters $\left(\frac{1}{4}\right)$
1 quarter	= 15 minutes (15 × 4 = 60 min)
1 minute	= 60 seconds
1 week	= 7 days
1 month	= 30 or 31 days (except Feb 28/29)
1 year	= 365 (+1 when it is a leap year)
1 year	= 12 months
1 year	= 52 weeks
1 year	= 4 quarters $\left(\frac{1}{4}\right)$
1 quarter	= 3 months
1 decade	= 10 years
1 century	= 100 years
1 millennium	= 1000 years

Days

Monday

Tuesday

Wednesday

Thursday

Friday

Saturday

Sunday

Months

1- January (31 days)

2- February (28/29 days)

3- March (31 days)

4- April (30 days)

5- May (31 days)

6- June (30 days)

7- July (31 days)

8- August (31 days)

9- September (30 days)

10- October (31 days)

11-November (30 days)

12- December (31 days)

12 hour clock	24 hour clock
12.00 p.m.	12 00 (afternoon)
1.00 p.m. ⟶	13 00 (add 12)
2.00 p.m.	14 00
3.00 p.m.	15 00
4.00 p.m.	16 00
5.00 p.m.	17 00
6.00 p.m.	18 00 (evening)
7.00 p.m.	19 00
8.00 p.m.	20 00
9.00 p.m.	21 00
10.00 p.m.	22 00
11.00 p.m.	23 00
12.00 a.m.	24 00

Time

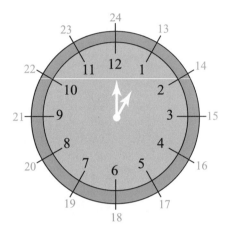

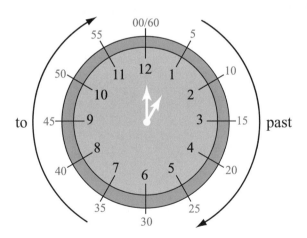

Time

It is 8.15, a quarter past eight or fifteen minutes past eight.

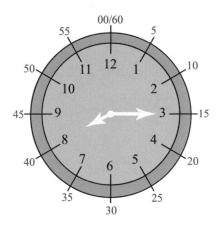

It is 8.35 or twenty-five minutes to nine.

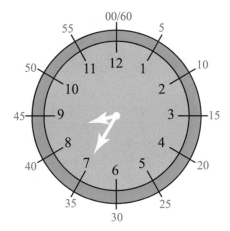

It is 3.25 or twenty-five minutes past three.

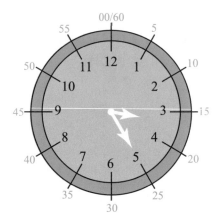

It is 3.45, a quarter to four or
fifteen minutes to four.

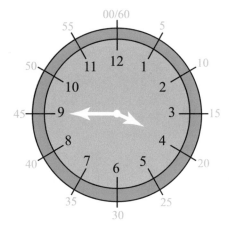

Time

1.10   ⟶   ten minutes past 1

4.30   ⟶   half past 4

8.20   ⟶   twenty minutes past 8

7.40   ⟶   twenty minutes to 8

9.50   ⟶   ten minutes to 10

6.55   ⟶   five minutes to 7

a.m. means: **ante meridiem (after 12 midnight till 12 noon)** morning

p.m. means: **post meridiem (after 12 noon till 12 midnight)** afternoon and evening

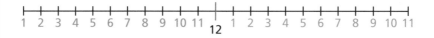

Time

A movie starts at 7.10 p.m. and ends 1 hour and twenty-five minutes later. At what time does the movie end?

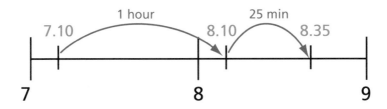

Step 1:   **7.10 + 1 hour** = 8.10

Step 2:   **8.10 + 25 min** = 8.35

The movie ends at 8.35 p.m.

Time

Emily took $2\frac{1}{4}$ hours to bake some cupcakes. She finished baking at 1.30 p.m. At what time did she start baking?

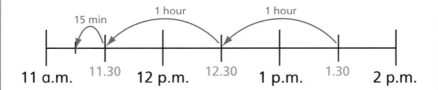

1.30 p.m. – 2 hours = 11.30 a.m.

11.30 a.m. – 15 min = 11.15 a.m. $\frac{1}{4}$ hour = 15 min

She started baking at 11.15 a.m.

time before 12p.m. will be in a.m.

Time, Speed and Distance

Time = Distance ÷ Speed

Ann lives 135 km away from Paul. If Paul travelled at a constant speed of 45 km/h, how many minutes would he take to reach Ann's house?

Step 1: Time = $\dfrac{\text{Distance}}{\text{Speed}}$ = $\dfrac{135}{45}$ = 3 hours

Step 2: Convert hours to minutes. 1 hour = 60 min
3 × 60 = 180 minutes

Paul would take 180 minutes to reach Ann's house.

Distance = Speed × Time

Speed = Distance ÷ Time

Length, Mass and Volume

1 km (kilometre)	= 1000 m (metre)
0.55 km	= 550 m multiply by 1000
1 m	= 100 cm (centimetre)
1 cm	= 10 mm (millimetre)

1 kg (kilogram)	= 1000 g (gram)
0.45 kg	= 450 g multiply by 1000

1 l (litre)	= 1000 ml (millilitre)
1.25 l	= 1250 ml multiply by 1000

Area of Rectangle and Square

length, 8 m

breadth, 3 m

The **area** of a rectangle is length × breadth.
The **area** of this rectangle is 8 m × 3 m = 24 m^2.

! Check: m × m = m^2 (square metre)

The **area** of this square is 36 cm^2.
What is the length of each side
of the square?

6 × 6 = 36   ! All sides of a square are equal.

The length of each side of the square is 6 cm.

Area of Triangle

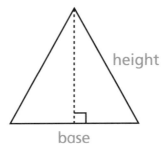

Area of triangle $= \dfrac{1}{2} \times$ base $\times$ height

$= \dfrac{\text{base} \times \text{height}}{2}$

Example:

The base is 5 cm and the height is 8 cm.

$\dfrac{1}{2} \times 5$ cm $\times 8$ cm $= \dfrac{1}{2} \times 40$ cm² $= 20$ cm²

The area of the triangle is 20 cm².

$\dfrac{1}{2} \times 40 = \dfrac{40}{2} = 20$

! Check: cm $\times$ cm $=$ cm²

Area of Circle

Area of circle = π × radius × radius

(The value of pi is 3.14; pi is written as the Greek letter for p: π)

So, area of circle, $A = \pi r^2$

Example:

The diameter of a circle is 14 cm. What is the area of the circle?

Radius of the circle: 14 cm ÷ 2 = 7 cm

Area of the circle

$= \pi$ × 7 cm × 7cm

= 3.14 × 7 cm × 7 cm

= 153.86 cm²

The area of the circle is 153.86 cm².

! Check: cm × cm = cm²

Perimeter

length, 8 m

breadth, 3 m

Perimeter of the rectangle

= length + breadth + length + breadth

= 8 + 3 + 8 + 3 = 22 m

---

length + breadth = $\frac{1}{2}$ perimeter   divide by 2

If the perimeter of a rectangle is 30 cm and its length is 6, what is its breadth?

6 + ? = 30 ÷ 2

6 + ? = 15

The breadth is 15 − 6 = 9 cm.

! Check your answer: 9 + 6 = 15. 15 × 2 = 30

Ratio (1) – *Counters*

	%/Fraction	Ratio
	Proportion of purple is 80%. $\frac{4}{5}$	Green : Purple 1 : 4
	Proportion of green is 33.3%. $\frac{2}{6} = \frac{1}{3}$	Purple : Green 2 : 1 simplified from 4 : 2
	Proportion of green is 75%. $\frac{6}{8} = \frac{3}{4}$	Green : Purple 3 : 1 simplified from 6 : 2
	Proportion of purple is 60%. $\frac{6}{10} = \frac{3}{5}$	Green : Purple 2 : 3 simplified from 4 : 6

Ratio (2)

Ratio means the total amount shared between individuals with different amounts each.

Jamila won $80 and treated his 5 classmates, Jim, Kevin, Joyce, Irene and Mildred, in the ratio 1 : 6 : 3 : 2 : 4. How much did each classmate get?

$1 + 6 + 3 + 2 + 4 = 16$, each unit is $80 ÷ 16 = $5

Jim: $1 × \$5 = \$5$
Kevin: $6 × \$5 = \$30$
Joyce: $3 × \$5 = \$15$
Irene: $2 × \$5 = \$10$
Mildred: $4 × \$5 = \$20$! Check: $5 + 30 + 15 + 10 + 20 = 80$

Ratio is the relationship between 2 groups of people, represented by 2 numbers.

The ratio of the number of teachers to the number of students is in the ratio 1 : 30. If the school has 1200 students, how many teachers there are?

$1200 ÷ 30 = 40$ teachers   ! Check: $40 × 30 = 1200$

Ratio and Proportion

A class has 42 students altogether. 24 of them are boys. What is the ratio of the number of boys to the number of girls?

42 − 24 = 18   18 of them are girls.

Boys : Girls

  24   :   18   *write in its simplest form,*

   4   :   3   *look for the common factor (÷ 6)*

These are the ingredients needed to make 8 chocolate chip scones.

260 g flour   50 g sugar   90 g chocolate chips

100 g butter   1 tsp baking powder

$\frac{1}{4}$ tsp baking soda   180 ml milk

How much chocolate chips, milk and sugar are needed for 20 chocolate chip scones respectively?

Chocolate chips: 20 ÷ 8 = 2.5, 2.5 × 90 g = 225g

Milk: 20 ÷ 8 = 2.5, 2.5 × 180 ml = 450 ml

Sugar: 20 ÷ 8 = 2.5, 2.5 × 50 g = 125 g

Average (1)

Formula: Average = $\dfrac{\text{total number or amount}}{\text{number of items/people}}$

4 students scored goals for soccer:

Sam :   1 goal

Neil :   0 goals

John : 6 goals

Tom :   1 goal

Total number of goals scored

$= 1 + 0 + 6 + 1 = 8$

Number of people = 4

Average = $\dfrac{8}{4}$ = 2 $8 \div 4 = 2,\ !$ Check: $4 \times 2 = 8$

The average number of goals is 2.

Average (2)

The table below shows the amount of money students from Class 5b spent on lunch in their school canteen. What was the average amount of money each student spent?

Food item	Price	Number of students
Chicken rice	$3	12
Sandwich	$2.50	4
Noodles	$2	12

$3 × 12 = $36

$2.50 × 4 = $10

$2 × 12 = $24

Total amount of money spent

= $36 + $10 + $24 = $70

Number of students = 12 + 4 + 12 = 28

The average amount of money each student spent was $\frac{\$70}{28}$ = $2.50.

$70 \div 28 = \$2.50$

! Check: $28 \times 2.50 = 70$

Algebra (1)

a, *x* and *y* are unknown numbers.

Adding:

$a + 2a = 3a$ $(a = 1a)$

Subtracting:

$6a - 4a = 2a$

Multiplying:

$x + x + x = 3x$ (compare with $4 + 4 + 4 = 3 \times 4$)

$(x = 1x)$

Dividing:

$6a = 72$

  $a = 12$ $(72 \div 6 = 12)$

Solving:

$3y + 8 = 26$ each side minus 8

$3y = 18 \longrightarrow y = 6$ $18 \div 3 = 6$

Algebra (2)

Find the values of a, b, c and d given that
$a = 4$, $b = 5$, $c = 3$ and $d = 8$.

Question	Solution
$a + b = ?$	$4 + 5 = 9$
$b + d = ?$	$5 + 8 = 13$
$d - a = ?$	$8 - 4 = 4$
$b - c = ?$	$5 - 3 = 2$

Note: ab means $a \times b$.

Question	Solution
$ab = ?$	$4 \times 5 = 20$
$\frac{d}{a} = ?$	$\frac{8}{4} = 2$
$ab + bc = ?$	$20 + 15 = 35$
$3c = ?$	$3 \times 3 = 9$
$b^2 = ?$	$5 \times 5 = 25$
$4b^2 = ?$	$4 \times 25 = 100$

Algebra (3)

x^2 = x to the power of 2
x^3 = x to the power of 3

x	x^2	x^3
1	1	1
2	4	8
3	9	27
4	16	64
5	25	125
6	36	216
7	49	343
8	64	512
9	81	729
10	100	1000

x^2 = x times x
Examples: (5 × 5), (8 × 8), etc.

x^3 = x times x times x
Examples: (5 × 5 × 5), (8 × 8 × 8), etc.

Algebra (4)

Square root: $\sqrt{}$
Cube root: $\sqrt[3]{}$

$\sqrt{}$	x	$\sqrt[3]{}$	x
$\sqrt{1}$	1	$\sqrt[3]{1}$	1
$\sqrt{4}$	2	$\sqrt[3]{8}$	2
$\sqrt{9}$	3	$\sqrt[3]{27}$	3
$\sqrt{16}$	4	$\sqrt[3]{64}$	4
$\sqrt{25}$	5	$\sqrt[3]{125}$	5
$\sqrt{36}$	6	$\sqrt[3]{216}$	6
$\sqrt{49}$	7	$\sqrt[3]{343}$	7
$\sqrt{64}$	8	$\sqrt[3]{512}$	8
$\sqrt{81}$	9	$\sqrt[3]{729}$	9
$\sqrt{100}$	10	$\sqrt[3]{1000}$	10

Example: $\sqrt{16} = 4$ because $4 \times 4 = 16$

Example: $\sqrt[3]{512} = 8$ because $8 \times 8 \times 8 = 512$

Money

$5.95 + $3.99 + $1.98 + $6.90 = ?

Method 1:   First rewrite, then add together.

```
        5 . 9  5
        3 . 9  9
        1 . 9  8
  +     6 . 9  0
  ─────────────────
  $  1  8 . 8  2
```

Method 2:   Round off each number to the
             nearest whole number.

$$
\left.
\begin{array}{l}
5.95 \ = \ 6.00 - 0.05 \\
3.99 \ = \ 4.00 - 0.01 \\
1.98 \ = \ 2.00 - 0.02 \\
6.90 \ = \ 7.00 - 0.10
\end{array}
\right\} +
$$

$19.00 – $0.18 = $18.82

add both columns first, then subtract the cents